NATURAL DISASTERS

Two Plays

By Jack Heifner

★

★

**DRAMATISTS
PLAY SERVICE
INC.**

SOUND EFFECTS RECORDS

The following sound effects records, which may be used in connection with production of these plays, can be obtained from Thomas J. Valentino, Inc., 151 West 46th Street, New York, N.Y. 10036.

TROPICAL DEPRESSION: #4070 — Thunder and rain
#4022 — Ocean waves

TWISTER: #5006 — Wind
#5033 — Explosion

NATURAL DISASTERS was first presented on the New York stage on January 28, 1985 at the West Bank Cafe Theatre. The lighting was designed by William Armstrong, the costumes by Patrick S. Wiley, the stage manager was Harrison Reiner and the production supervisor was Christie Harrison. The West Bank Theatre is under the direction of Steve Olson, Lewis Black, Randy Foerster and Rusty Magee. The play was directed by Diane Kamp. The original cast was as follows:

TROPICAL DEPRESSION

GLORIA................................. Patricia Miller
JANINE................................. Sally Sockwell
JIM DUPUI .... Rusty Magee
MEL...................................... John Wojda

TWISTER

BETTY.................................. Sally Sockwell
ROY .... John Wojda

The World Premiere production of TROPICAL DEPRESSION took place on June 3, 1984 as part of the Texas Playwrights Festival at STAGES in Houston, Texas. The play was directed by Ted Swindley. The cast was as follows:

GLORIA............................. Sally Edmundson
JANINE .... Nancy Lee Rogers

This play is dedicated
to my first teacher in the theater and my lifelong friend,
Jerry Worsham.

CONTENTS

AUTHOR'S NOTE

These two plays are part of a group of four one-act plays I have written on the subject of "home." The other two plays are PATIO and PORCH. Whereas TWISTER examines the relationship of a husband and wife and TROPICAL DEPRESSION is about two friends; PATIO deals with two sisters and PORCH is the study of a mother and daughter. Any of these plays may be done alone or together, since their subject matters are related. However, the two plays which make up the evening called NATURAL DISASTERS share another bond. The catalyst for each is a disaster (a tornado and a hurricane) and the realizations brought about by such events.

PATIO/PORCH is also published by Dramatists Play Service.

TROPICAL DEPRESSION

TIME

A week during the winter of this year.

PLACE

The balcony of a hotel room somewhere on a remote island in the Caribbean.

CHARACTERS

GLORIA
JANINE

Both women are Texans and are in their early thirties.

SETTING

There's a balcony railing across the front of the stage. On the balcony are a couple of chairs and a table, with a colorful cloth in a tropical print. A door leads from the balcony to the hotel room. In the background there is the silhouette of a palm tree. The sky in the background should change colors for each new scene.

OTHER PRODUCTION NOTES

Music, sound effects and properties are indicated in the script.

The play requires five fast costume changes for the women.

In the New York production, a live combo was used to bridge the time between scenes. This consisted of a piano player/singer, Jim DuPui, and a bongo player, Mel. They created the mood of "Happy Hour" at the hotel with songs and some improvised dialogue. The show opened with Jim singing the song "Tropical Depression." (Words to this song are included in the back of this script. Music to this can be composed by the individual production.)

TROPICAL DEPRESSION

SCENE ONE

*The sky is blue and the time of day is late afternoon. Gloria,
after having trouble opening a stuck door to the balcony, enters.
She is expensively dressed and, despite the heat, wears a fur
coat. After looking out at the view, Gloria turns and yells off-
stage.*

GLORIA. Oh, my God! It's too much! Too much beauty!
Darlin', put those bags down and come look.
JANINE. *(Her voice coming from off-stage.)* For heaven's sake,
you'd think they'd have somebody to help carry my stuff up four
flights of stairs!
GLORIA. *(Rushing around the balcony.)* Janine, you're not going to
believe this!
JANINE. I can't believe you booked me into this fleabag
hotel.
GLORIA. Honey, I know you've never seen anything like this in
Houston. *(She takes off the coat.)*
JANINE. I've never seen a room like this in my life!
GLORIA. Janine, get out here!
JANINE. *(Rattling the door to the balcony.)* I'm trying!
GLORIA. What the hell are you doing?
JANINE. I'm trying to open the door to the balcony, but it's stuck.
*(Gloria crosses to open the door, but the door handle comes off in
her hand.)*
GLORIA. Just push on it. *(Janine pushes on it and finally the
door opens.)*

JANINE. *(Entering. She's beautifully dressed and also wears a fur coat. She carries a train case.)* For God's sake.

GLORIA. Who needs a door handle anyway. *(She tosses the handle off the balcony.)*

JANINE. *(Sitting.)* I want you to know, I may have broken a finger nail.

GLORIA. *(Excited.)* Honey, forget about your nails and just look. *(She grabs Janine and pulls her to the railing.)*

JANINE. Just look at what?

GLORIA. *(Pointing off the balcony.)* You can't tell me you've ever seen anything as gorgeous as that big, blue harbor ... or that big, blue pool ... or *that* big, blonde lifeguard! I think we should rush down to that pool, right now, and drown. Lifeguard! Help! Help! *(She laughs.)*

JANINE. *(Paying no attention to the view.)* Gloria, this can't be the best hotel on this island. Isn't there a Sheraton or a Hyatt we could move to? *(Taking off her coat.)*

GLORIA. Sweetheart, it's the height of the season and the Eden Isle Club sounds so classy. Like a country club.

JANINE. But since when is the "penthouse suite" a fourth floor walk-up with one room and a balcony?

GLORIA. Oh, but it's a charming terrace. And isn't this a nice touch. *(She crosses to a bouquet of flowers and a bottle of champagne on the table.)* Flowers and a bottle of champagne! Compliments of the management, no doubt.

JANINE. I doubt it.

GLORIA. *(Reading the card.)* "To My Miss Texas ... Miss You Already, Love, Murdock." Love, Murdock? Well, I guess these were wired ahead for you. You're the only ex-beauty queen on this balcony and the only one of us married to Murdock.

JANINE. Oh, how sweet. Frankly, you should have known this hotel wouldn't give us flowers and champagne ... they won't even spring for a bellboy.

GLORIA. And I should have known my husband wouldn't think of sending me anything to brighten my arrival, except maybe our divorce papers.

JANINE. Oh, Gloria ... now you know Bucky adores you. He gives you everything your little old heart desires, including that big new house you've been dying for.

GLORIA. Darlin', the man's as excited as I am about having separate bedrooms.

JANINE. The man's a saint. How many other guys would love your kids ... from all your marriages ... as if they were his own?

GLORIA. He likes it a whole lot more when I ship the little boogers off to my mother's.

JANINE. I don't know why you're always running him down.

GLORIA. And I don't know why our husbands want to go off to their deer lease every year and shoot themselves silly for a week. I intend to spend every penny Bucky's got. He's going to pay dearly for every damn deer he brings back and stuffs in my freezer.

JANINE. I think Bucky's wonderful.

GLORIA. But he's no Murdock. Flowers, champagne ... your husband's a romantic fool.

JANINE. Tell me about it. I'm worn out.

GLORIA. And that's why we're here, darling. Screw those clowns! We're on vacation. Just us girls!

JANINE. Oh, I wish poor Charmay could have come. It doesn't seem the same without her. Maybe we should have stayed and seen her through her time of need. *(She exits into the bedroom.)*

GLORIA. I will not deal with any guilt as far as Charmay is concerned. It was her choice to use deer hunting season as the time to have her new face installed. Not me, baby. When I have my cosmetic surgery, Bucky's gonna sit right there with me. If he wants his wife to look eighteen again, he's gonna hear every scream I scream.

JANINE. *(Entering with another train case.)* Oh, I could just cry.

GLORIA. Darlin', Charmay needs a new face worse than a vacation.

JANINE. I mean, I could just cry about this crummy hotel. Charmay chose such lovely places for us to stay in Aruba last year and Cancun the year before. Besides, I thought you said we were going to Barbados ... then I thought you said we were going to Bermuda

11

... and we've ended up in some God forsaken spot called Barbuda.

GLORIA. Oh, Janine... where's your spirit of adventure? Dolores said this is just one in a series of remote islands in the British West Indies. We're actually in what's known as the Lesser Antilles.

JANINE. Well, Dolores should go back to selling Tupperware instead of bad trips. I'm sure if Charmay had organized this trip we'd never had ended up in the "Lesser" Antilles.

GLORIA. Would you shut up about Charmay.

JANINE. I think I'll get a glass and have some champagne *and* try and forget where I am. *(She exits to get a bathroom glass.)*

GLORIA. Besides we're not going to spend very much time in our room.

JANINE. *(Entering and going to the champagne.)* God, I hope I don't break another nail opening this bottle.

GLORIA. *(Scattering out a pile of brochures.)* So what'll we do first?

JANINE. Do? I thought we came here to relax? *(Janine gets the champagne open and drinks some during the following. She drinks it down like water.)*

GLORIA. *(Reading the brochures.)* Now it says here that there's a Happy Hour every day down by the pool featuring Jim DuPui and his combo, The Pieces of Eight. *(Looking off the balcony.)* Oh, it looks like Jim's only got one piece of eight. Oh, well, that's a great place to go, sip a drink and stare at the lifeguard.

JANINE. He's not that cute.

GLORIA. He's adorable. Oh, and look... we can take this "World Famous Surry Ride" and view the entire island. See? *(She holds up a brochure.)* And I have a feeling the duty free shopping is incredible. I can buy all sorts of things for my new house. Oh, with all these things to see and duty to do ... well, I don't know where to begin. I want to play — play! Shop — shop! Spend — spend!

JANINE. *(Who has been looking into the room from the doorway.)* There's no TV in our room!

GLORIA. T — V! TV? Oh, for heaven's sake, you're not here to watch TV.

JANINE. What if I get bored?

GLORIA. You won't get bored! However, I saw one down in the lobby when we were checking in. If you must watch, then I guess you'll have to go down there and mix with the natives.

JANINE. You know, when we were driving in from the airport, I noticed what I consider to be a lot of poverty. I thought for awhile we'd flown all the way here to go to shanty town.

GLORIA. Sweetheart, that's what's known as local color. It's divine!

JANINE. And the sky is so blue. Too blue. Doesn't it hurt your eyes?

GLORIA. Honey, I want to remember that color for my new powder room. It's sensational!

JANINE. And is that awful room air conditioned? It's incredibly humid here.

GLORIA. Darlin', this is the tropics! Natives and poverty and pool boys! It's paradise!

JANINE. It's the pits! In fact, it's not at all what you promised. *(She exits again.)*

GLORIA. Darlin', I only promised you a good time and a good tan. In fact, that's the main thing we have to do. Get brown. So, we'll get up tomorrow and go to the beach. Oh, but before that, we can have the Continental.

JANINE. *(Entering with another make-up case.)* What are you talking about?

GLORIA. *(Holding up a brochure.)* Well, it says here: "The Dining Room serves Breakfast from 7:30 to 10 a.m. Continental Breakfast from 10 to 11." It's included in the price of our room ... all our meals are.

JANINE. But I'd like to be at the beach by 10. The morning sun is the best sun, and if I can't be there by then ... then I'd rather not go at all.

GLORIA. Okay, fine ... who wants the Continental anyway? Knowing you, you'd probably order the Continental Breakfast and then say, "Oh, and no bun, please."

JANINE. You're absolutely right ... buns are not on my diet.

GLORIA. I just thought we should eat something if we want to stay at the beach all day. We'll miss lunch.

JANINE. Fine. Then let's go to the big breakfast. I'll eat fruit.

GLORIA. Fine. Then we'll get up at eight. Is that too early?

JANINE. I don't know.

GLORIA. Is that too late?

JANINE. Well, normally if I have to be someplace, I have to be up at least two and a half hours before hand.

GLORIA. *(Getting irriatated.)* Before ten or before you go to breakfast?

JANINE. Well, let's go at nine.

GLORIA. Nine?

JANINE. Let's eat at nine, then come back to the room, change clothes and be at the beach by 10:15.

GLORIA. Christ, so we're getting up at 6:30?

JANINE. You said eight.

GLORIA. *(Screaming.)* I thought you wanted more time! That only gives you an hour to do whatever it is you do do in the morning. Hell, Bucky can get up ... shit, shower and shave ... and be out the door in half an hour.

JANINE. Well, I'm not Bucky. I like to ease into my mornings. Funny, but I've been on the same schedule ever since I was in the pageant.

GLORIA. Funny, but that was years ago.

JANINE. If I alter my routine ... I'll fall apart.

GLORIA. Okay, fine ... you just let me know when you've pulled it all into place and are ready to face the world.

JANINE. Fine. So what are you going to wear to the beach? I mean, should I wear full regalia there and then take it off?

GLORIA. Just throw some shorts on over your bikini.

JANINE. Bikini? Have you lost your mind? You know very well I don't own a bikini. They never allowed them in the pageant and once you get used to competing in a one-piece, it's very hard to adjust to a bikini. In fact, I still have the very Catalina suit I wore when I won. Shall I wear it tomorrow?

GLORIA. I'm sure that's just the thing. However, I don't see any reason to get too done up. It's all very casual here ... so why don't you just leave your crown in the room. *(Music is heard. A man is singing from the pool area of the hotel.)* Listen ... just listen. I think Happy Hour has started! *(Breaking into song.)* "Feelings ... la, la, la, la ... Feelings ... "

JANINE. What a sad song for Happy Hour.

GLORIA. "Feelings ... la, la, la, la ... Feelings ... "

JANINE. I wish I hadn't had so much of this champagne ... I must have a bit of a hangover. Maybe it's from all those high-balls I had on the plane. Actually, I think it's from last night. Murdock insisted we have a private little going away party.

GLORIA. How sweet. Bucky didn't even tell me good-bye.

JANINE. So we drank a lot and the two of us never got around to having dinner.

GLORIA. Oh, that's so romantic.

JANINE. What's so romantic about passing out?

GLORIA. *(Pointing off the balcony.)* Oh, Lord ... he's getting up and going over to the bar to get a drink. God, Janine ... look at those legs! Big muscles bulging out. Look at those arms! Big muscles bulging out. Look at that tiny swimsuit. Big ... bulging ...

JANINE. *(Pointing.)* Look at that Pina Colada!

GLORIA. Come on, let's go downstairs and see him up close. We're going to Happy Hour, girl. *(She's exits to the bedroom.)*

JANINE. I can't go like this! I have to change clothes and freshen my make-up. I'm all crumpled from the flight.

GLORIA. *(Rushing on ... she's changing into another outfit.)* If you take two and a half hours to get dolled up for Happy Hour, we're gonna miss it! Nobody cares how you look.

JANINE. What a terrible thing to say to a former Miss Texas!

GLORIA. Well, we're off to a great start. I'm going to Happy Hour. You do whatever you like. *(She exits again.)*

JANINE. I'm going to put on something appropriate before I go downstairs. You never know who you might run into. What if I happened to see someone from Houston at cocktail hour and they saw me in anything less than my Oscar de la Renta cocktail dress?

GLORIA. *(Rushing in, dressed for Happy Hour.)* It would be a

15

tragedy, Janine.

JANINE. It most certainly would be.

GLORIA. *(Singing.)* "Earrings... nothing more than earrings... "
*(She rushes to get her purse, grabs some earrings out of it, puts them on
and rushes out. Janine pours some more champagne and then opens one of
her make-up cases. She reaches in and pulls out her Miss Texas crown.
The lights fade and tropical music is heard.)*

SCENE TWO

*The tropical music fades as the lights come up. The sky is red
and the two women are bathed in red light. They are seated in
the chairs. Both women wear large beach towels. They do not
move and there's a long pause before they speak.*

JANINE. I'm in such pain. I can't remember ever experiencing
such pain ... except maybe when I lost in Atlantic City.

GLORIA. *(Muttering under her breath.)* Jesus.

JANINE. I wonder if this feels anything like what Charmay is
going through with her skin?

GLORIA. Oh, hell no. They've got her so doped-up on Demerol,
she probably can't feel any thing.

JANINE. Do you have something stronger than a valium? I've
taken six and I'm still too nervous to look at myself in the
mirror.

GLORIA. Take a couple more. I think I'll call-up the lifeguard
and have him bring up a bottle of Mazola. Then we'll just pour it in
the tub and sit in it.

JANINE. I think alcohol may be the answer.

GLORIA. Pour alcohol on us?

JANINE. No, in us.

GLORIA. Maybe I should stand up. *(She tries to stand, but screams
in pain and falls back into her chair.)* God, my legs feel so horrible

when they rub together.

JANINE. That's because you fell asleep in the sun spread eagle. It was not a pretty sight.

GLORIA. Christ, there's got to be something to ease this grief.

JANINE. *(Holding up a bottle of lotion.)* Did you use this green stuff?

GLORIA. *(Going for it and rubbing some on.)* I'll try anything.

JANINE. It's called "Aloha Aid."

GLORIA. "Aloha Aid?" What does it do? Help you say "good-bye?"

JANINE. You know, today we've not done many things.

GLORIA. Today we've done nothing but try to stop screaming over our skin. *(Music from Happy Hour is heard.)*

JANINE. We could go down to Happy Hour. I could use a Pina Colada.

GLORIA. Do you have any idea what time it is? Is it dinner time?

JANINE. We've got loads of time before dinner. Time does not fly in the tropics. Gloria, why do you think it's so hot here? Despite the cool tropic breezes, the sun is incredibly hot. Why don't the cool breezes cool down the heat? Nor does the sun heat-up the cool ocean breezes. They're two things co-existing, but do not mix. They're totally segregated. Like the rest of this island. Don't you think?

GLORIA. I don't want to think about it. Let's just try to have a good time.

JANINE. A good time? Look at us!

GLORIA. We are not a pretty sight. I suppose we'd better just skip dinner and stay in our room this evening.

JANINE. We should be in the hospital. We should have stayed in Houston with Charmay and had our faces done. I don't know what to do. Just go to sleep? Sleep it off?

GLORIA. I guess so.

JANINE. Gloria, I wonder if there's anything I can do to wake up in the morning and feel good?

GLORIA. Yes ... kill yourself tonight. *(The lights fade. Music begins.)*

SCENE THREE

The lights come up on Gloria sitting on the balcony. She is surrounded by shopping bags. She gets up and goes into the room to get something. Music from Happy Hour continues. When Gloria re-enters she accidentally shuts the door.

GLORIA. Oh, shit. *(She sits down again. The sky in the background is pale blue, yellow and lavender. We hear a sound from the room.)* Janine, honey ... is that you? Somehow that door got closed. *(After pushing on the door several times it opens. Janine enters.)* Where have you been?

JANINE. Oh, I was just downstairs in the lobby watching TV.

GLORIA. Funny I didn't see you there when I came in.

JANINE. Have you been shopping ever since you left me on "The World Famous Surrey Ride" this morning?

GLORIA. Indeed I have.

JANINE. When did you get back?

GLORIA. Oh, about a half hour ago. I've just been looking at all my divine purchases and enjoying our spectacular view! Happy Hour's in full swing. Did you drop by there?

JANINE. I told you I was watching television.

GLORIA. Jim DuPui sang "Feelings" twice. Then he sang "Can't Help Loving That Man." I thought that was unusual.

JANINE. Bold, to say the least. How many unhappy people are at Happy Hour today?

GLORIA. No one's showed up yet and my big blonde's not on duty at the pool. I wonder where he could be? I was just about to get up enough nerve to go down and attack him ... and he's not even around. Not that anyone would want me at this point. My face can

18

only be compared to the look of an old, cracked alligator bag.

JANINE. I know. I spent a good hour peeling mine this afternoon then slapped some Alaha Aid on it and screamed Bloody Mary.

GLORIA. Oh, Happy Hour's stopped. I guess Jim's going on a break. Oh, well ... c'est la vie!

JANINE. La vie!

GLORIA. You know, I'm so proud of us.

JANINE. What'd we do?

GLORIA. Well, after two days of sitting in the room playing Old Maid and hanging around the hotel taking pain killers ... today we finally got out and took that goddamn "World Famous Surrey Ride." Unfortunately, it wasn't the blast I'd hoped for.

JANINE. I rather enjoyed that mountain top place we stopped at, with the enchanting birds and those enchanting banana dacquiris.

GLORIA. You must have been enchanted. You threw back four there and then got two more to go.

JANINE. It was just like a movie. I could see Bali Ha'i rising out of the ocean and Mitzi Gaynor singing "Some Enchanted Evening."

GLORIA. Hell, you had more to drink than I thought.

JANINE. You know, when I was in the pageant, I sang and twirled to a medly from South Pacific.

GLORIA. Twirled? I didn't know you twirled.

JANINE. Only on occasion. People who saw my act said I sang much better than Mitzi Gaynor.

GLORIA. I'm not sure that's saying a hell of a whole lot, but I'll tell you one thing, I really took a disliking to our "World Famous Surrey Tour" guide this morning.

JANINE. Me, too. I couldn't understand a word he was saying. What language do they speak down here?

GLORIA. English.

JANINE. Really? Well, it doesn't sound a thing like the English we speak at home. Therefore, to keep myself occupied, I was just talking to that fat woman sitting next to me ... trying to tell her about me ... when he up and shouts at me, "Madame, I will try to point out the beauties of this island if you will try to shut-up about being a beauty queen." I decided I'd better be quiet or else I'd end up on a bar-be-que stick.

GLORIA. Oh, darling ... he was mad at me long before that.

JANINE. I know, he warned you we were only stopping in town for ten minutes and you shopped for half an hour.

GLORIA. *(Pulling some prints out of a shopping bag.)* There was a long line in the gift shop and I had to get these native prints. I thought they'd add a little color to my new entry hall. I had no idea he'd up and leave me.

JANINE. He waited for you forever. Finally, he just gave up. We were halfway down the hill before you came running out with your shopping bags, screaming ... "Honey, honey ... stop that god-damned surrey." I've never been so embarrassed. *(They laugh.)*

GLORIA. Did you want him to leave me?

JANINE. No ... of course not. But you could have stopped shopping.

GLORIA. I came here to shop. At least I convinced him to drop me off downtown instead of bringing me back to the hotel with the rest of you.

JANINE. I think he was relieved to get rid of you.

GLORIA. The feeling was mutual. But I did get some divine things in town. Lots of straw mats and shit for my rumpus room. And I found a fabulous antique shop. Wait 'till you see my major purchases. I got myself real fine art works. *(She's pulling things out of shopping bags.)* I don't know where I'm going to put everything. I especially think this is cute. *(She puts a small table on the floor.)*

JANINE. What is it?

GLORIA. It's a national treasure of China.

JANINE. Then what's it doing in Barbuda?

GLORIA. Oh, God! Bucky's gonna kill me and I hope one of the kids doesn't jump on it.

JANINE. Is it a foot stool?

GLORIA. I guess. All I know is I spent seven thousand pounds on something that "looks like" a foot stool.

JANINE. Seven thousand pounds? What's that in dollars

and cents?

GLORIA. I haven't any idea, but since a pound weighs much more than a dollar ... I figure I got much more than I paid for.

JANINE. Are you sure you haven't been taken for a fool?

GLORIA. Absolutely not! This stool was a bargain compared to some things in that gallery ... 25,000 pounds for some old red ashtray. Well, I suppose it wasn't an ashtray when some old civilization made it centures ago, but that's what I'd use it for.

JANINE. Thank God you stopped yourself from buying that.

GLORIA. I'll probably go back and get it tomorrow. I loved it!

JANINE. What's this pile of other things? They look like old, broken baby dolls.

GLORIA. Oh, they are. They're Santos figures from the cathedrals of Spain and Portugal. They're A.D. Little bitty baby Jesus figures for the small guest room, and for the primitive feeling I want in the dining room, I got this adorable Ecuadorian fertility figure. She's B.C. *(She holds up a clay figure.)* That's before Christ. Christ, I don't even know what goddamn religion I'm dealing with.

JANINE. Well, you certainly did make a haul.

GLORIA. I certainly did. Charmay is going to be green with envy. She's always going on an on about how it's taken her years to put together her fine art collection. I bought all mine this afternoon. Twenty minutes max! *(Music is heard.)*

JANINE. Oh, Happy Hour's started again. It was such a success for the last three hours that Jim decided to extend it. *(They laugh.)*

GLORIA. Every afternoon, I look forward to hearing that music sort of wafting up here. I know all of Jim's routines by now. I can even sing harmony with him. I sing off the balcony—like Juliet to my blonde Romeo.

JANINE. I hate to admit this whole trip's been rather humorous. We've got sacks of fine art works and a sink full of dead skin in the bathroom.

GLORIA. "Peelings ... la, la, la, la ... peelings!

JANINE. Oh, Gloria!

21

GLORIA. Darlin', I love the tropics! I feel simply divine! You just can't rest like this in Houston. Well, maybe you can ... but me, with Bucky and the kids ... and this year after beating Charmay out of the Presidency of the Junior League ... well, my dear, I just run myself silly all the time.

JANINE. I'm plenty busy with Murdock.

GLORIA. But you know, it's like we're such good friends and yet we don't ever get a chance to talk. There's something I've been meaning to ask you. It's sort of a question out of the blue.

JANINE. Guess what? I'm very good at "pop" questions. I scored the highest of any contestant when they asked me a very hard question in the finals.

GLORIA. Which was?

JANINE. "What advice would you give someone who is trying to become a beauty queen?" And you want to know what I answered?

GLORIA. I can't wait.

JANINE. My advice to someone who wants to be a beauty queen is ... "The you that you are ... is better by far ... than the you, you are trying to be."

GLORIA. What in hell does that mean?

JANINE. Well, I suppose it means be happy ... be satisfied with what you have.

GLORIA. Oh, Janine ... where did you get that answer? Out of a Cracker Jack box?

JANINE. I made it up and the neat part was that I rhymed by accident. The judges thought it was very clever.

GLORIA. And it is ... but what I was wondering about has more to do with the future than the past. I'm just curious as to when you and that sexy tycoon of yours are going to start a family. You've been married ... what nine or ten years?

JANINE. I don't know.

GLORIA. Charmay and I have had your baby shower on hold for ages.

JANINE. I'm in no hurry. I've told you before, Murdock and I can't seem to get things going together. God knows, Murdock

22

keeps trying to make babies all the time ... he never lets up. Like you, this may also be the best rest I've had in years. I certainly have forgotten how nice it is to be alone for awhile.

GLORIA. Alone? I'm here.

JANINE. I know ... but that's not what I mean. I guess the only time I was ever really on my own was the year I traveled around during my reign ... opening supermarkets and playing Rotary Clubs. Of course, I had a chaperone but for that one year ... I was just me ... Miss Texas. Then, after I was replaced, the invitations stopped. I married Murdock. I didn't know what else to do. It's like I was given only one perfect year in my life. It was a celebration of me. Ever since then it's like I've just been filling time.

GLORIA. I know what you mean. I have so many responsibilities to my fund raising, my clubs, my classes. I'm booked up being a fabulous, professional, non-working woman. But you know ... last night I was just standing here. You were already asleep. And that ship in the harbor was all lit up with strips of white lights. And the fires from the native huts up in the hills of Barbuda were twinkling in the background. It was all so beautiful and quiet and peaceful. I can't sit in my backyard at home and look out at anything like this. All the money in the world can't build or buy this view. It should all be so simple. God, I loved those white lights. It's no wonder I like twinkle lights so much on my tree at Christmas.

JANINE. I guess both of us have all the clothes and money and everything a girl could want. Right?

GLORIA. I guess. Oh, but look at that sky. Pale blue, pale yellow ... Directoire colors. The water is all silver and the clouds lavender.

JANINE. You must recreate this as a mural in your new dining room.

GLORIA. Do you think so? Do you think the kids would like it?

JANINE. I don't know anything about what kids like. *(There's an awkward pause.)*

GLORIA. Well ... neither do I.

JANINE. Well ... *(Music from Happy Hour begins.)*

GLORIA. *(Breaking the mood.)* Maybe we should go downstairs to dinner.

JANINE. *(Changing moods also.)* Oh, barf! Do we have to eat here again?

GLORIA. Yes ... it's part of the deal we're paying for.

JANINE. How can you spend 7,000 pounds on something that "looks like a footstool" and then worry about the cost of a dinner? Besides, the food's terrible and it takes forever to get waited on.

GLORIA. *(Lighting a cigarette.)* I'll tell you what. Let's go into town and find someplace wild.

JANINE. I'd like that.

GLORIA. Let's put on our serious boogie-woogie dresses, try to salvage our faces and go knock this island on its ass.

JANINE. I can be ready in an hour if I set my mind to it.

GLORIA. I'll give you fifteen minutes max. Enough of this leisure shit! We're gonna paint that puny little town red! *(They laugh ... Gloria, without realizing it, has pulled a red ashtray out of a shopping bag ... she flicks her cigarette in it. Then both Janine and she notice what she's bought.)* Oh, my God! I bought it! *(They laugh as they start to exit. The lights fade and music begins.)*

SCENE FOUR

The lights come up on Janine, out on the balcony. She is having a drink and is already a bit tipsy. Music is coming from the Happy Hour. Jim is singing a popular song. The sky in the background is grey and purple ... storm clouds. Janine wears her crown and a cape with a long train. She is singing along with Jim and when the song stops she starts yelling to him.

JANINE. *(Yelling off the balcony.)* Jim, I'm over here! Look! Fourth floor ... here, over here, Jim! Let's sing another one!

24

GLORIA. *(Entering, very upset… she has many more shopping bags.)* What the hell are you doing? *(She slams the door to the balcony.)*

JANINE. You yell off the balcony all the time!

GLORIA. I take a short shopping trip and you make a fool out of yourself.

JANINE. Short? You've been gone all day. What old junk did you haul back this time?

GLORIA. Never mind what I've bought. I'm so upset right now, I can't see straight. That lifeguard is sitting down in that lobby watching T.V. I kept looking at brochures, asked for messages, bought some cigarettes … I did everything you can legally do in a lobby to waste time. He just stared and stared.

JANINE. So why'd you come upstairs?

GLORIA. I couldn't figure out a reason to mill around any longer. God, what do I have to do to get him? He knows where I live … he knows my balcony … and still, he doesn't come up. Why does he just keep staring?

JANINE. Maybe, he can't believe how blatant you are. You watch him like a vulture the entire time he's at work. That's no way to get a man. Come on, let's go back downstairs … we'll go to Happy Hour. I need another drink.

GLORIA. A drink? Oh, God, I don't want another Pina Colada as long as I live.

JANINE. I had seven this afternoon.

GLORIA. Seven? Janine, after you got so sick on them last night?

JANINE. It wasn't because of the Pina Coladas, I got sick. It's because I had too many of them. As much as I've pooh-poohed fruit drinks in my life, you can really get into them down here. I don't even remember leaving that nightclub we went to.

GLORIA. I remember because I ran into a wall.

JANINE. I do recall at some point you were up onstage singing Christmas Carols and doing a dramatic monologue about your new house.

GLORIA. I did that?

JANINE. Rum drinks have a tendency to fool you or make a fool

25

out of you. I threw up all night.

GLORIA. And I lost my new sunglasses ... nothing happened to you except you threw up. I lost my favorite thing in the world. They were beautiful.

JANINE. Who needs 'em? I think it's going to rain.

GLORIA. Oh, I could just cry. *(She's about to.)*

JANINE. Why are you getting so upset about a little rain?

GLORIA. It's not the rain! It's that lifeguard, damn it!

JANINE. Oh, he's not so great. In fact, he's real stupid.

GLORIA. Honey, I assume he's stupid. I don't care about his mind.

JANINE. He's one of those people who only talks shop. The only thing he knows about is sun and water and chlorine.

GLORIA. *(Frantic.)* How would you know? Have you been talking to him? What did he say? *(Suddenly, there's thunder and lightning.)*

JANINE. What's going on?

GLORIA. When did you talk to him?

JANINE. Heavens, it's getting dark so fast.

GLORIA. What did he say?

JANINE. Gloria, look ... don't those clouds seem huge?

GLORIA. *(Grabbing Janine.)* Tell me about the lifeguard!

JANINE. Look! Those are the biggest clouds I've ever seen!

GLORIA. Janine, answer me! *(Thunder, lightning... Janine runs for the door.)*

JANINE. Oh, my God, it must be a hurricane! We'd better get inside! *(They both head for the door. Thunder, lightning ... a scream from the two women as they try to open the door.)* You idiot! Why'd you slam the door when you came out here?

GLORIA. I was so furious about Blondie, I didn't know what I was doing.

JANINE. *(Rushing to the railing.)* I can't believe we're stuck out here! Help! Help! Everybody at Happy Hour must have run for cover. Look ... is there anyway to get from our balcony to the one below us?

GLORIA. No, no ... I didn't buy a rope!

JANINE. You could jump to the ground or try to leap for that mango tree!

GLORIA. I'm not about to commit suicide trying to save our lives! *(Thunder and lightning.)*

JANINE. Help! Help! Where's that damn lifeguard when you need him? He's probably picked up somebody else in the lobby and they're off in his room! *(She doesn't realize what she's just said.)*

GLORIA. What the hell are you talking about/

JANINE. *(Now realizing ... she covers.)* Nothing ... help! Help!

GLORIA. Answer me! Are you so damned drunk you don't know what you're saying? *(She chases Janine across the balcony.)*

JANINE. *(Angry.)* I'm not drunk! If you had any sense about anything, other than buying out Barbuda you could have slept with him, too!

GLORIA. *(Screaming.)* Slept with him? Too? My God! He went to bed with you? When?

JANINE. Yesterday ... today ... everyday while you've been out shopping!

GLORIA. What'd you do? Use that worn-out Miss Texas "charm act" of yours on him? Did you wear him down, like you do the rest of us, with one complaint after another about the weather, the hotel room, the way you look?

JANINE. *(Screaming back.)* I'm a hell of a lot more interesting to talk to than you are! All you know to talk about are your damn silly decorating schemes.

GLORIA. How dare you! *(Pause.)* How was he?

JANINE. Fabulous!

GLORIA. I could murder you! *(Gloria goes after Janine ... thunder, lightning, rain begins ... Janine runs away.)*

JANINE. What difference does it make if I had him? It's all you've talked about doing all week.

GLORIA. I may have talked about it, but I wouldn't have done it! I'm a happily married woman!

JANINE. Happy? You're happy? Who's happy? You spent all of Bucky's money on trash, well, I blew Murdock's on the lifeguard.

GLORIA. You paid for him?

JANINE. I charged him! He takes American Express. Why do you think guys like him work at hotels ... for the joy of fishing people out of the pool? *(Thunder, lightning ... Gloria and Janine look out, suddenly seeing how terrible the storm is.)*

GLORIA. Oh, God ... I'm going to die in a monsoon! They're going to find my waterlogged, burnt-up body out on this balcony ... with you!

JANINE. Somebody help me!

GLORIA. You keep on screaming, honey. I intend to pray.

JANINE. Help! Help!

GLORIA. *(On her knees at the railing.)* "Our father who art in heaven ... " *(Thunder, lightning.)*

JANINE. Maybe I can make it to that mango tree.

GLORIA. *(Really scared.)* Don't leave me. I'm afraid. *(Thunder, lightning ... Gloria is crying.)*

JANINE. *(Calmer, opening up to Gloria.)* Come on, huddle close to me, Gloria. Don't worry ... we'll make it through. *(She takes her cape and uses it to shield them from the rain.)*

GLORIA. Janine, you'll ruin your royal robe.

JANINE. It's okay. *(They huddle together.)* You know, I never thought I'd share this with anyone. *(They smile at each other, then look out at the storm ... the lights fade. Thunder, lightning ... the storm fades and we just hear the sound of the ocean.)*

SCENE FIVE

The lights come up on Janine, alone on the balcony. She is dressed in a sarong made out of a native print. This should be the same fabric that once covered the pillows on the chairs on the balcony or was the tablecloth on the table. Everything else has been wiped away by the hurricane. The sky behind the

28

balcony is filled with stars. There's a pause, then Gloria enters. She wears a matching sarong.

JANINE. Did you get a call through to Bucky?

GLORIA. Finally. I asked him to pay for our new plane tickets and to meet us at the airport tomorrow. I guess we should pack tonight.

JANINE. Pack? Pack what? Everything we own must be scattered all over beautiful Barbuda. I hope they have a cold spell here so those natives get to wear those minks.

GLORIA. But Janine—look! *(Pointing off the balcony.)* That Mango tree survived and I'll swear that looks like your Oscar de la Renta cocktail dress dangling from the top of it. Should we fetch it?

JANINE. No. Let it be. Frankly, those ruffles look like hell of a lot better on that tree than they ever did on me. Besides, I'd rather just stay in our room. I've become rather attached to it ... literally. *(They laugh.)*

GLORIA. Me, too. *(A sigh.)* God, I can't believe I'll be arriving back in Houston tomorrow having spent thousands of dollars of my husband's money and sporting nothing more than a sarong and the ugliest specimen of human skin ever.

JANINE. I guess we should have gone to what's left of the dining room tonight, for old times sake. Needless to say, after the monsoon, they were serving a seafood buffet.

GLORIA. It seems they've set up an improvised bar by what once was the swimming pool. Do you want to go down to what they are loosely calling "Happy Hour" for a farewell Pina Colada?

JANINE. No ... not really. This is me, for once, turning down a drink.

GLORIA. I wonder where Jim is?

JANINE. I think hurricane Heidi probably swept him out to sea.

GLORIA. I'll bet he was singing "Ebb Tide" as he floated away. *(They laugh.)* And I haven't seen your blonde lifeguard about, but then I suppose when he saw the storm approaching he just grabbed his surf board, his bleach bottle and his considerable life savings and rode a wave off into the sunset.

JANINE. Gloria, are you very angry with me?

GLORIA. I still can't believe you did that.

JANINE. I'm sorry, but I didn't do it to hurt you and I didn't mean to tell you. I guess I just can't stop competing. And I guess I wanted to see what it felt like to buy somebody ... to pay for somebody's affection. That's what Murdock is doing to me. He bought himself a Miss Texas just because he thought I was pretty. Now he wants me to have kids. So he's offered me a fur coat and a new car if I'd have one. He doesn't understand ... I have five fur coats ... four, and a year old Mercedes. I've got everything ... but somebody who loves me for who I really am. But then who am I really?

GLORIA. I can't answer that question about myself. I know I really do love Bucky. He's building me that new house to try and make me happy. And I keep myself as busy as I can ... always trying to outdo Charmay. I guess we're all in competition. And I don't give myself a minute to devote to my marriage, because ... the truth is, I'm a lousy wife and mother. I've got three marriages and three kids who hate me to prove that. Bucky's the best man I've ever known and I'm going to lose him if I don't start loving him. I've got to stop bitching and spending and settle down.

JANINE. Do you think you can do it?

GLORIA. I don't know. But I just can't do what I've done before.

JANINE. Maybe I should stop being Miss Texas. *(Pause.)* It's going to be awfully hard to let her go.

GLORIA. You want to know one thing really nice about this vacation?

JANINE. Tell me one thing.

GLORIA. You've become my best friend, Janine.

JANINE. Better than Charmay?

GLORIA. Much better than Charmay. And sometimes what a girl really needs is a best friend.

JANINE. Sometimes that's just about all a girl has. Thank you for a wonderful time, Gloria.

GLORIA. You'd better mean that ... 'cause if you tell anybody, especially Charmay, that we didn't have a wonderful time down here ... I'll kill you. *(They laugh ... the ladies put their arms around each other ... as the lights fade.)*

THE END

TWISTER

TIME

Early evening ... shortly after the tornado.

PLACE

A pile of rubble that once was a tiny Texas town.

CHARACTERS

ROY— A trucker in his early thirties.
BETTY— His wife ... slightly younger than Roy.

SETTING

The tornado has blown a door, a ladder, a piece of a fence, some clothes and assorted other objects into a pile upstage. There is something about the arrangement of these objects that is rather beautiful; as if nature has created a piece of "junk sculpture." Behind this is the open sky, which should change colors for each new scene.

OTHER PRODUCTION NOTES

Sound effects and properties are indicated in the script. In the New York production of the play, music was used to cover the transitions between scenes.

TWISTER

SCENE ONE

As the auditorium goes dark, sounds begin. Wind, explosions, crashes pierce the darkness. Lightning flashes. A woman is heard screaming in the darkness. A dim light comes up onstage and we see Betty. She is running back and forth. She wears tight pants, a halter top and very high mules. Her face, hair and clothes are covered in mud. As she runs about the stage, she continues to hit her head with her hands.

BETTY. Help me! Help me! Won't somebody help me?

ROY. *(From off-stage.)* Betty? Come out, come out, wherever you are. *(Roy suddenly appears. He wears a torn shirt and a pair of jeans. The seat is torn, exposing his boxer shorts.)*

BETTY. *(Not seeing him.)* For God's sake, where is everybody?

ROY. *(Exhausted.)* Betty! Betty, honey! I've found you at last!

BETTY. Can anybody hear me? *(There's no response to Roy as she continues to hit her head. Roy grabs her and she lets out a scream.)*

ROY. Oh, Betty, baby!

BETTY. Roy? Good Lord, Roy... I didn't know if you were dead or alive!

ROY. Oh, darlin'... I didn't know if you were either! And you look like a mess. I ain't ever seen you this dirty.

BETTY. What?

ROY. But we're both alive! That's what's important. Thank you, Jesus!

BETTY. *(She stands staring at him.)* Well, speak up, Roy. Don't just move your mouth. What's the matter with you?

ROY. What are you talking about?

BETTY. This is no time to play games. Speak up!

ROY. Oh, baby ... what's happened?

BETTY. What?

ROY. Can't you hear me, honey?

BETTY. *(Scared.)* Roy, now stop that! *(She hits her head again.)*

ROY. Good God, you've been blown deaf!

BETTY. Oh, no, Roy! Oh ... I think there's a distinct possibility I may be deaf?

ROY. What?

BETTY. What? *(They're both upset and a bit frantic.)*

BOTH. What?

ROY. Darlin', look at my lips. *(She's looking the other direction. He suddenly grabs her face with his hands and holds it so that she must look at his face ... then he yells.)* Look ... at ... my ... lips!

BETTY. What the hell are you doing?

ROY. I'm moving my lips ... so watch!

BETTY. *(Screaming.)* Are you crazy? I told you, I can't hear! Let go of my face! Squeezing my cheeks ain't gonna help my hearing! Oh, God, there's roar in my head like freight train's running loco thru my brains! How did this happen?

ROY. Oh, my Lord, honey, how *did* this happen?

BETTY. Roy, aren't you the least bit concerned about how this horrible thing happened to me?

ROY. Yes, yes.

BETTY. You remember that tree over by the grocery store? *(She looks at him.)* Well, nod yes or no!

ROY. Yes! Yes! *(He nods his head.)*

BETTY. Well, I ran to that tree and threw myself down. *(She acts this out as she describes it.)* I held onto some big roots on each side, but the wind was blowing so hard that I could hardly hold on at all. Can you hear me?

ROY. *(Nodding "yes".)* Yes ... yes. You haven't lost your voice!

BETTY. Anyway ... there I was with these huge roots in my

hands ... when I saw the grocery store fly apart! The whole store just kinda lifted up off its foundation and sighed. It hung there in the air for a minute and I swear it sighed ... went "ah." It tilted a little, went "ah" again, then it exploded ... and food and crap went all over the place!

ROY. Oh, Lord ... what are we going to do without the grocery store?

BETTY. It was then that I saw this terrible thing coming! It was black and it was dipping up and down, heading right at me. First it started slapping me around the tree in one direction and then in the other. Next it would suck me up ... then throw me back down. At one time, my feet would be almost straight up in the air, and another time it would bang me right into the ground. I remember that my mules were about to come off and so I kept on working my feet because I didn't want to lose my shoes for some crazy reason.

ROY. Good thinking!

BETTY. You probably think that's silly, but I thought it was good thinking on my part. But the worst was yet to come and that started when the water hit me!

ROY. Water?

BETTY. Remember that low spot behind the tree that was always filled with about two and half feet of dirty water? The twister pulled the slush out of that hole and threw it at me! And you remember all that gravel that was on the street? Remember?

ROY. *(Nodding "yes".)* Sure ... sure.

BETTY. Well, honey, that came next! There used to be truckloads of gravel there ... two or three inches deep ... and all of it was flung right at me! Look at me Roy!

ROY. *(Yelling.)* I am looking! You are filth, darlin', from head to toe! You've got muddy water all over you and lots of small rocks in your ears.

BETTY. Help me, honey.

ROY. *(Going to her.)* My poor baby. Daddy's gonna make it all okay. Just relax. *(He begins to pick the rocks out of her ears.)*

BETTY. Ooh! Ouch! Be careful.

ROY. Easy, now ... easy.

BETTY. Hurry! You know I can't stand anything in my ears... not even a Q-tip.

ROY. Hold still! looks to me like you could have picked these pebbles out yourself, but you've always been sort of helpless.

BETTY. What?

ROY. You've got all kinds of mess caked up in here ... mud, hair spray, chicken feathers and God knows what else.

BETTY. Would you hurry!

ROY. I'm done, darlin'. I think you're all cleaned out. *(He screams in her ear.)* Can you hear me?

BETTY. *(She grabs her head.)* God, that's so loud!

ROY. Wait a minute ... I think I missed something. Let me get it! Just calm down. *(Betty makes sound as Roy tries to get the rock... he gets it and says.)* Lookie here ... it's a big purple rock.

BETTY. *(Disgusted.)* You idiot! That's not a rock, that's my ear bob ... put that back on!

ROY. *(He clips it back.)* Sorry. Now is that better, Betty?

BETTY. I guess so. I suppose it was just a temporary loss of hearing caused by all those rocks and the emotional stress involved.

ROY. Good.

BETTY. Good? Do you know how it feels to have rocks in your ears?

ROY. No.

BETTY. Do you know what it's like to be hit by a truckload of gravel?

ROY. No.

BETTY. It's like being stoned, Roy. Stoned! It's like the Christians in the Bible, honey. I've been stoned!

ROY. Well, sugar ... I'm sorry.

BETTY. You should be. Where the hell were you when I needed you? I was hanging on to a tree for dear life, and you were out running around, having a good time.

ROY. I was not. I told you this morning at breakfast I was going over to Powell.

BETTY. Powell?

38

ROY. I was on Highway 22, in the truck, going over to Powell to pick up a load of tomatoes.

BETTY. Tomatoes?

ROY. I told you that Tuesday I was going over to Powell and get those tomatoes and on Friday I was going to haul squash.

BETTY. Squash? They don't grow squash in Powell. What do you take me for? Squash in Powell. Don't make me laugh.

ROY. No, no ... I get the squash in Poteet, but the tomatoes come from Powell.

BETTY. *(Shouting.)* Well, be clear! You don't seem to understand that I have just been assaulted by a tornado and I am not in the best frame of mind.

ROY. *(Irritated.)* Well, I was hit, too! I had to deal with that funnel the same as you.

BETTY. You couldn't have experienced anything remotely resembling the tragedy that I have suffered.

ROY. It was worse for me.

BETTY. No way. It could not have been. You're standing there clean as a whistle and I'm all covered in mud; and you have the gall to tell me you've been through more misery than me? Huh?

ROY. Did that tornado chase you?

BETTY. Don't be silly.

ROY. Well, she did me.

BETTY. Oh, don't be silly. Funnels sort of dip or lolly-gag about. They don't chase.

ROY. This one did. I'd look in the rear-view mirror and there she'd be ... right on my tail. I'd take a turn or two ... look back ... and she'd still be right on my behind.

BETTY. So?

ROY. So finally I got out and ran across a field. I thought she just wanted the rig 'cause she shook it to pieces. It's scattered all over creation!

BETTY. You lost the truck?

ROY. I didn't lose it! She took it ... sort of ate it up, spit it out and then she came after me! She snatched me up by the seat of my pants! See! *(He shows where the seat of his pants is missing.)* I was yanked up by the butt and carried about a hundred yards then she dumped me smack dab in the middle of some telephone lines. There I was hanging in the air like some fool high wire act at the circus!

BETTY. Is that all?

ROY. No, no... I was hanging there until the wires snapped in two and I fell right down to the ground. That must have been when all the phone service went out, because I tried to call you. I stumbled round with my poor aching butt until I finally got to the Texaco station out on the highway. I wanted to call you and warn you that the tornado was a coming.

BETTY. Well, I wasn't home anyway.

ROY. It seems you were out hanging onto some tree.

BETTY. You talk like I had planned to spend my afternoon doing that.

ROY. What were you doing out?

BETTY. I was going to the grocery store.

ROY. What for?

BETTY. For food, silly.

ROY. You should've stayed home. I could have prevented you from getting all those rocks in your ears, if I could have warned you.

BETTY. You couldn't have told me nothing. Not if you knocked out all the phone lines. Use your head! And I'll tell you one thing. I'm damn glad I got out of the house.

ROY. Oh, you always find some excuse to get out of the house.

BETTY. Well, it was a smart move on my part.

ROY. Well, whatever. Come on now... let's go on home and get you a bath.

BETTY. That's why it was a smart move on my part, Roy. We are home.

ROY. Home? Here?

BETTY. It was here, Roy, but it blew up, too.

ROY. Blew up?

BETTY. That rotten old house didn't last five minutes in that wind, honey.

ROY. This can't be home.

BETTY. Now, sweetheart, you know where the Kingdom Hall used to sit?

ROY. Of course I do.

BETTY. And what used to sit next door to the Kingdom Hall?

ROY. Our house.

BETTY. You notice I said, "what used to sit." I said that because it don't sit here no more. I'm telling you when I got up ... let go of my roots ... I tried to come home but there wasn't anyplace to come. I've been running around here trying to find where it blew to ... but it's just not to be found.

ROY. I don't believe you! It's gotta be around here someplace. It's just gotta be. *(He rushes off.)*

BETTY. Roy, there's no need to go looking for something that's gone. You're wasting your time. You could pick your teeth with what's left of that house! Roy, wait for me! *(She rushes off after him ... Blackout.)*

SCENE TWO

A short pause ... then lights up. Roy stands looking straight front. Betty stands beside him. A pause.

ROY. It's so depressing. It's just gone.

BETTY. I hate to say I told you so ... but I told you so.

ROY. Well, I don't know what to do.

BETTY. Frankly, honey, I never liked that old house much. It was an ugly shack.

ROY. It was my family home. Most of my family was born here. Died here. I had always intended to die here.

BETTY. And you would have ... we would have both kicked the bucket if we'd been home, but we weren't and now it's gone. Poof! Gone with the wind.

ROY. I kept saying eventually I'd do this or someday I'd do that to the house... you know, add on... extend the place. Build us an extra half a toilet. I never dreamed the whole thing would just blow off.

BETTY. *(Very matter of fact.)* Well, it did.

ROY. Fire ... yes. I thought about that. Remember me talking about how a fire could wipe a person out?

BETTY. *(Unconcerned ... she's beginning to clean the mud off her face.)* No.

ROY. Explosions always worried me ever since the hot water heater blew up over at the school house. Blew those little kids up, but not away. Not like this. Remember?

BETTY. No.

ROY. Floods never worried me. Ain't no river or creek big enough around here to cause a flood. But this "thing" ... this whirlwind ... just whipped in, then out... and now there ain't nothing to paint or fix or add onto no more.

BETTY. Nope. It's just like in the Wizard of Oz, Roy. I'll bet parts of that house are in Oz or Kansas or all the way up in Dallas, for that matter.

ROY. It's a crying shame. I mean, I'm looking at what used to be the view from our front porch ... except there ain't no porch. There ain't even a view!

BETTY. Well, there never was much of one, really. So cheer up, Roy! For crying out loud, it's not the end of the world.

ROY. *(Something dawning.)* Well, maybe it is. Maybe that's it.

BETTY. What's it?

ROY. Maybe this is the end. Do you realize we ain't seen another living soul.

BETTY. You can live for years in this silly town and never see another soul. We have always had a quiet, lonely life stuck out here in the middle of nowhere.

ROY. I really think this is the end of the world as we knew it and I'll just bet the Lord has chosen us to the last two people on earth.

BETTY. Oh, please. Why in God's name would the good Lord

choose you and me to be the last? We never even darkened the doors of that goddamned church.

ROY. I know, but I've always been told that the Almighty is a pretty sneaky guy.

BETTY. But he's no fool. He wouldn't choose us under any condition. No matter how desperate he was.

ROY. You know, maybe he's left us here to be the brand new Adam and Eve.

BETTY. Oh, don't be kinky, Roy.

ROY. I think it's a plan ... to start anew ... a new creation.

BETTY. There's one catch Roy. Look around you. Do you think this is the new Eden? Eden, honey, was famous for being a piece of paradise. This here, honey, is a pile of poop.

ROY. Poop? Looks like there's some nice things here.

BETTY. Besides, I am sure God wouldn't want me to be the New Eve. And I'm not even positive I want to be the New Eve. Eve was supposed to be fruitful and multiply ... populate the whole world.

ROY. So maybe God's gonna get you going at last and suddenly we're gonna have a pile of babies.

BETTY. Oh, calm down. This is not the end of the world or a new creation. This is a tornado. And I ain't about to start birthin' babies out right and left. I'm too tired to have kids.

ROY. *(Excited.)* I'm beginning to see it clear! First, famine ... then flood ... then locusts ... and now, tornado! This is just one in a series of Biblical disasters. It's like the plague.

BETTY. It's like the worst. And it ain't the end, Roy. We're the same two people. We're still alive and kickin'.

ROY. Oh, no.

BETTY. Oh, no ... what?

ROY. Maybe we're not. Maybe we're dead and this is the waiting room to hell, honey.

BETTY. Honey, what exactly is all this junk doing in hell's waiting room?

ROY. Waiting. Maybe God scooped up all the shit in the world and plopped it down right here. Maybe this is the world dump.

What do you think?

BETTY. *(Irritated.)* I don't want to think about it.

ROY. Unless ... oh, my heavens ... just unless, we're in the Twilight Zone.

BETTY. *(Suddenly scared.)* Don't say that!

ROY. We may be on the outer reaches of man's imagination.

BETTY. Shut up, Roy.

ROY. We are now entering another dimension. Nee-nee-nee-nee.

BETTY. Stop it, Roy. *(She points to the ground.)* Look! This is earth, Roy. This is the same old earth we've been on all our lives. This ain't Mars or Eden or Twilight ... this is Texas. We're smack dab in the middle of the same hick town! So hush up with your silly ideas.

ROY. *(Slightly defeated.)* Well, I don't know what to do.

BETTY. Don't do anything. Get your mind off this mess. I'm pulling myself back together. I've found a few things to fix myself up with— somebody's odd colored lipstick, a splash of "Evening in Paris", and a peach blusher. But what I wouldn't give for my own eyelash curler.

ROY. You're right. We may have lost the house, but I guess we're fortunate that there are other things that can't be blown off. Birth certificates, marriage license, our papers. those are all in the bank in a safety deposit box. Plus we've still got some money there. It's lucky for us that all that stuff's over at the bank. Safe and secure.

BETTY. Honey, I have one more thing I feel I must tell you. Our stuff's not likely to be there.

ROY. It's there. Nobody can open that box at the bank and take anything out without me being there.

BETTY. Well, there ain't much point in having a box at the bank ... 'cause it blew off, too.

ROY. *(Screaming.)* Oh, dad blast it!

BETTY. Don't yell at me. I didn't blow the bank away.

ROY. Are you sure it's not there?

BETTY. I have surveyed the mess and it's vanished.

ROY. But we've got to have our papers. If they're not in the bank, then where are they now?

BETTY. Where do things go? Somewhere over the rainbow, I suppose. *(She begins to sing to herself. She pays no attention to Roy.)*

ROY. What the hell are we going to do? Without that stuff we can't even prove we were born or married. We don't even have a penny to our names. That bank's just gotta be there! *(Rushing toward the exit.)* It's just gotta be! *(He exits.)*

BETTY. *(Turning around, then realizing he's gone.)* The bank! Roy, we didn't have more than ten dollars in the bank anyway. It's not like we lost our life savings, since we didn't have any! *(Rushing off in a different direction.)* Roy, don't you leave me here! *(She exits .... Blackout.)*

SCENE THREE

A short pause... Then the lights come back up. Roy stands surveying the scene. A pause.

ROY. Oh, God.

BETTY. *(Her voice coming from off-stage.)* Oh, Roy—there you are. I've been looking all over for you.

ROY. Oh, God.

BETTY. *(Entering.)* Now, now, Roy ... it could be worse.

ROY. Worse? There really is nothing left out there. I couldn't even find where the bank sat. *(He points off stage.)*

BETTY. *(Pointing in the other direction.)* Well, there's a reason for that. What little's left is that pile of bricks right over yonder by that other pile, which was once the grocery store. See that bent-up Co-Cola sign?

ROY. *(Pointing.)* Right there? Are you sure?

BETTY. Sweetheart, I have walked this street a million times, .

45

back and forth to that store to get your supper or me a magazine. I know all too well the layout of this pitiful place.

ROY. Seems to me the bank was back over there. *(He points off in the other direction.)*

BETTY. No, no ... that was where the old school house was. See where that twisted teeter-totter has landed?

ROY. There?

BETTY. Yes, well that was the school. *(She points at several other places.)* Then over there sat the Kingdom Hall, see that one splintered pew? This was our house ... and there were two other homes down at the end of the road. Old lady Higgin's house was about where that chimney is and I don't see Ed Blakestone's place at all, but that looks like his beat-up Dodge coupe. That's where everything was, Roy, I know.

ROY. I guess everything and everybody's been blown sky-high!

BETTY. I know that, too. I watched it all happen.

ROY. *(Pacing about.)* Oh, Lord ... this really is a disaster.

BETTY. That's a most accurate observation, Roy.

ROY. I wonder where the Red Cross is? And where's the National Guard when you need them? I always thought the Governor rushed down and helped the victims in times like these.

BETTY. Oh, I'm sure they'll all be here sometime soon. They probably can't find us on the map.

ROY. I sure hope somebody knows we've been hit.

BETTY. Well, I sure can't turn on the TV and find out if we made the news. I'm just sick about missing all my programs this afternoon. I'll probably never catch-up on the story lines. You miss one day of "As The World Turns" and you have lost out, baby. What are you doing?

ROY. *(Digging in the rubble.)* I think maybe I could try to dig up a CB and call somebody or build a fire and send smoke signals. Or better yet, let's draw a big S.O.S. in the dirt just in case some plane flies over.

BETTY. Oh, calm down. If you don't stop acting like some overgrown Boy Scout, you're gonna have a heart attack.

46

ROY. *(Screaming.)* I can't be calm. This is without a doubt the worst day of my life. I've lost my home, my town, my truck, all my money. I'm beside myself.

BETTY. And I'm pooped. *(Sitting… taking off her shoes.)* My feet are killing me! These dogs are barking, baby. I'm gonna sit and relax.

ROY. How can you relax at a time like this? We've got to get busy.

BETTY. Busy? Busy doing what?

ROY. I'm sure not going to sit around. I think we should try and put this town back together—and start to build some sort of shelter.

BETTY. We should just wait. Sit and wait for help. It's like running out of gas on some deserted road. You wait and sooner or later someone comes along. You don't get out and build a town because you're out of gas.

ROY. It looks to me like everything sort of blew off that-a-way. I'll bet some of our stuff is over there.

BETTY. So?

ROY. So we ought to look for what's ours.

BETTY. What for?

ROY. Because it's ours.

BETTY. I really don't want none of it. Frankly, I feel sort of glad that it's all gone.

ROY. How can you say that?

BETTY. Because we had so much junk and there's been many day when I've prayed for something to wipe it all away. Take it away! So I don't have to dust it, wash it, wipe it no more. This is like a miracle to me!

ROY. Well, not to me. I'm going to try and dig up some of my things.

BETTY. And how do you think you are going to recognize "your things?" What makes you think your things look any different from anybody else's stuff?

ROY. I know what's mine. *(He exits. During the following he will go off and come on several times. Each time he brings back a few items. Betty*

47

continues talking, even when he's off-stage. He only hears bits of her conversation.)

BETTY. We all shop the same store, since we only had one. Everybody's everything looks just like everybody else's and ain't none of it pretty. You just buy whatever they got. And around here you live thinking that all dishes are melmac ... and towels are gifts that come in detergent boxes ... and soap is Ivory. Ain't got no way to question why that soap is what it is and that's 99 and 44/100 percent pure. I mean, what's the 50 something percent that ain't pure? *(Roy enters.)* It could be 50 percent poison or 50 percent nothing.

ROY. That's pure shit.

BETTY. It may be! They don't let you know! I might as well be living in Russia, with the Communists! *(Roy exits again.)* I see all those products on TV ... brand after brand ... and I can't get them. I long to squeeze the Charmin just once. I want to sit in the beauty shop and hear Madge say "You're soaking in it!" I'm just dying to put a package of Parkay on my kitchen table and hear it say, "Butter." But what can I get here? They sell toilet tissue, dishwashing liquid and margarine. You can't squeeze it or soak in it or carry on a conversation with it.

ROY. *(He enters. He holds up a girdle, a bra and a pair of panties.)* Lookie ... I think I found some things of yours. Your drawer full of women's things must have blown off over there. There's a whole slew of your panties. I found Monday through Friday, except the ones that say Tuesday. I hope you've got those on.

BETTY. Throw that stuff back!

ROY. But it's yours. I saw you wear this thing. *(Holding up a bra.)*

BETTY. Roy, this may come as a shock to you, but many women wear those things.

ROY. Not a stuffed one like this! This is your living bra.

BETTY. *(Angry.)* Throw it back! Kill it! I don't want it.

ROY. *(Putting some of his things down.)* Well, I'm going to pile my things over here. *(He exits again. Betty picks up a scarf and ties it around her head. She finds some make-up to put on during the following.)*

48

BETTY. I guess the funny thing is ... if I'd known this thing was going to hit I would have taken the time to put on something else. I guess I would have gotten dressed up, "done up" for the disaster. I think I would have put on my new purple pantsuit I just finished sewing. The one that was so difficult to make from that Simplicity Pattern. I know I wouldn't have chosen to wear what I've ended up in. *(Roy has entered again with more stuff.)* This outfit don't even match.

ROY. That's what you always wear when you go to the store.

BETTY. That's right. That's where I was going. *(Roy exits.)* I had been watching TV. I remember that Dinah was on Merv ... or maybe Dinah was on Donohue? Anyway, she was singing some song ... I believe it was "The Way We Was." And I had just wondered whether she was singing that because she was still upset about Burt Reynolds. I wondered if Dinah was going for some hidden meaning. Whether she was just working out her problems with a song ... just her and the band. Then this commercial came on for Franco-American little Ravioli pies. ·Cutest little things. I thought maybe you might like them for your supper. Something different. So I got up ... leaving Dinah with her thoughts about her confused love life ... put on my go-to-the-store outfit and went out the door.

ROY. *(He has entered again.)* Well, it's good to know it's something you feel comfortable in. I, myself, always wear just about the same thing. Men don't have TV watching outfits and go-to-the-store outfits. Men don't change.

BETTY. Boy, you don't have to tell me.

ROY. I'm having luck. I've already found my hunting cap, my beer mug, my picture of Mommy and Daddy and my suspenders.

BETTY. Found any food?

ROY. Food?

BETTY. I've been hungry ever since I started to the store.

ROY. Well, don't touch anything that's not wrapped or in a can. There's some food scattered about, but it could be contaminated.

BETTY. I'm so hungry I could eat a horse.

ROY. Now wait ... I think I saw one over there.

BETTY. I don't really want to eat a horse, silly.

ROY. I think I spotted a can of stew around someplace. *(He is looking.)*

BETTY. Stew? Pugh! You know I hate canned stew.

ROY. Lookie here ... *(Finding something.)* It's a package of Hostess Snowballs! Ain't even been blown open. I know you like Snowballs because I've seen you eat them.

BETTY. Well, I sort of had my mouth set for something "not sweet."

ROY. You want to give that dead horse a try?

BETTY. I guess I'll have to content myself with a Snowball ... hand them here. *(He does ... she bites into one.)* I wish it was a Twinkie. Anything to drink?

ROY. Oh, Lord.

BETTY. These Snowballs are awfully dry. These taste like day old Snowballs. I'm gonna choke if I don't get something to drink.

ROY. Like what?

BETTY. Something like a Diet Dr. Pepper. *(She coughs.)*

ROY. God, you are particular. You're gonna have to drink whatever I can find. *(He is looking around.)*

BETTY. Well, I know what I like.

ROY. Wait ... now ... let's see ... here's a can of something.

BETTY. *(Choking on the Snowball.)* I hope it's a diet!

ROY. It's a Mountain Dew!

BETTY. Oh, for Pete's sake ... it'll do. I'd hate to think I survived the tornado and choked on a Snowball! *(He hands her the can of soda. She takes a swig and then belches.)*

ROY. Are you happy now?

BETTY. *(Taking another bite and a sip.)* Humm.

ROY. We should probably gather up all the food. Collect food.

BETTY. *(Really enjoying her snack.)* Hummm.

ROY. Looks to me like when the grocery store went poof ... most of the food sort of blew off that way. *(He rushes off.)*

BETTY. *(A pause... she takes another bite, puts on her shoes and walks off after him.)* Roy, you're going the wrong way! I told you the store was over there! If you start digging in the church rubble, you're not going to find me anything to eat except maybe a box of crackers and a bottle of Mogan David. Roy, are you listening to me? *(She exits ... Blackout.)*

SCENE FOUR

Short pause... then the lights come back up. Roy sits drinking a can of beer. Betty sits eating from a pile of cookies, Fritos, diet drinks. There's a long pause after the lights come up.

ROY. Let's put all the food over here ... this will be the kitchen area.

BETTY. Hummm.

ROY. If I can dig up a mattress... I can put it over there. That'll be the bedroom. And I'll put the bath over here.

BETTY. Why not put the bath over there? *(She points to the bedroom area.)*

ROY. Seems to me it should be here. *(He indicates the kitchen area.)*

BETTY. Why that's exactly the layout of our old house.

ROY. Right.

BETTY. Why not change things around? If I'm going to have a new bath, I want it here ... right by the bedroom.

ROY. But the bath was always off the kitchen. You could get up after eating and go straight to the bathroom.

BETTY. *(She stops eating.)* Whatever you say.

ROY. I figure it shouldn't take us too long to get set up again. I know it won't look just like home for awhile, but see here in the living room area? *(He moves to that area.)* I'll find all of your stuffed animals or get you some new ones. And I think I'll build a shelf to

51

put them on. I always wanted that instead of me having to sit with all of them on the sofa. Would that please you?

BETTY. *(She's disturbed.)* I don't know.

ROY. And next time I haul something down Mexico way, I can pick you up another one of those pictures of a bullfighter painted on velvet. You liked that, didn't you?

BETTY. Oh, I was getting sort of tired of it.

ROY. And don't you worry. I'll get you a new TV. I don't want you to have to miss another minute of "The Turning World" or whatever. Everything's gonna be fine, baby. This house is gonna look like it always did. We're gonna forget about this catastrophe and live like nothing ever happened.

BETTY. *(To herself.)* Nothing ever did happen.

ROY. I'm going to put the house back together ... starting right this minute.

BETTY. Oh, God ... no. Roy, wait. Just stop and listen to me for a second. *(He stops. She really tries to explain her feelings to him.)* Honey, remember when we first met? You came into that little place where I was working outside of Dallas.

ROY. V's Cafe?

BETTY. Yes ... V's ... and you came in there and ordered a steak. Not a little chopped steak, but the big one. The one on the menu that nobody ever ordered. I didn't even think we had it, 'cause nobody ever ordered such an expensive piece of meat.

ROY. But you had it.

BETTY. And I served it ... and I thought, this guy not only has good taste, but he must also have a wad of money.

ROY. And I thought you were just about the prettiest thing I had ever seen. I fell in love with you at first sight ... in that little white uniform of yours that was sort of too tight across your behind.

BETTY. *(Laughing ... they are sharing warm memories.)* Now, Roy ... it wasn't too tight. It was just sort of snug.

ROY. Whatever it was, it was awfully cute.

BETTY. And I thought you were kind of cute, too. I mean, you had that huge mother of a truck and you were hauling melons to market in Dallas.

ROY. There was money in melons.

BETTY. And when you offered me a ride back to my trailer court ... I just about died! I felt like I had made it!

ROY. Seems like I felt the same way. I mean, all the girls I had dated back here at home ... and there wasn't much of a selection ... but both of them were so boring to be with. But you ... well, I don't know. When we sat there outside of your little trailer ... relaxing in the sunshine. You in your bikini swimsuit ... chattering on and on about the stars in Hollywood and all the things you knew so much about. And we had some beers ... and you offered me some chip-and-dips ... then you rubbed my neck ... and well, I just felt like a king.

BETTY. And I guess I thought that what you were. I mean, when we started chatting, you were always mentioning your Mommy and Daddy and your family home ... and in my mind I guess I started picturing the Old South and some mansion like "Tara." I thought you were a rich landowner and there I was a simple waitress at V's. So when you popped the question later that night and we ran off and got married ... I thought I was bettering myself. I was moving up! Then you brought me here. Hauled me here. What a shock! That house of yours was a dump. Your mother and father were living in some sort of an ignorant bedridden bliss. I had to serve them all the time. I was worse off than when I was a waitress. They didn't even tip! I was fooled, Roy.

ROY. Not by me.

BETTY. No ... not by you, really. By my own dreams, I guess. I just wanted more and got less. This town ... that house ... oh, please ... let's just leave here, Roy.

ROY. Leave here? I think those rocks must have knocked the sense out of you.

BETTY. Or into me. I know it's silly to wish, to still dream at my age ... but I wish ... I wish that old funnel had just picked me up and sat me down someplace else. It was plain stupid of me to hold on to those roots. Hold on for what? For this dear life? Damn me! I missed my chance. I could have gotten a free ride out of here.

ROY. I have no desire to get out of here.

BETTY. But, Roy, everything is gone.

ROY. I gotta find what's left. If it's all gone, then what have I got?

BETTY. Me and a new start... a reason not to hold on to the past anymore. It's great, Roy!

ROY. Great?

BETTY. The cleansing power of it all. It's like being born again! So let's go! Roy, let's just run away!

ROY. But I'm putting my home back together.

BETTY. Honey, don't waste your time trying to set up a bathroom here or a bedroom there. For heaven's sake, don't try to put the whole joke back together!

ROY. *(Getting angry.)* Joke? I'm not going anyplace new.

BETTY. You won't leave with me?

ROY. No ... I don't want to. I want things the way they were.

BETTY. *(Her anger building.)* No way, Roy. I hated the way it was. If this hadn't happened, I'd be fixing your supper and we'd be eating fried chicken again ... because I was just dreaming when I thought the store might have those little Ravioli pies! Then we'd sit all night, like always. Until it was time to go to bed and get up and do the same thing all over again tomorrow. Good Lord, Roy, the only thing I've had to look forward to in years is the different guests Merv and Donohue had on every day. At least the guests change! Are you listening?

ROY. *(Gathering items to avoid thinking.)* I'm too busy.

BETTY. You're always too busy.

ROY. My job is here!

BETTY. Hauling? Roy, you can get a new truck and haul tomatoes anyplace. You don't have to live here to haul. You stayed here because of that damn house.

ROY. My Mommy and Daddy were here.

BETTY. Were, Roy... *were!* They're dead, you know. Dead for years. Gone! And now that house is gone.

ROY. You give me one good reason why you want to leave here!

BETTY. Because I never wanted to be here in the first place.

(Pause.) Roy, I wanted something nice ... I wanted a nice, pretty life.

ROY. Honey, you're all caught up in this world you see on TV or read about in your Harlequin Romance Books. That's not real. This is the real world right here. Living like we lived is what life's really like.

BETTY. It can't be, Roy. I've got to think there's a little more because I've been existing on almost nothing for so many years now. I've gotta get out of here while I've got a chance. Before I get stuck again.

ROY. All this is happening too fast for me.

BETTY. Tornadoes happen that way. They pick up lives and twist them about. Jumble people up a bit. Out with the old and in with the new. So are you going to come with me?

ROY. No.

BETTY. Then thanks for all the rotten memories, honey. I'll always love you, but I've got to go. *(She starts to leave.)*

ROY. Go where? Back to V's? Back to waiting tables? Is that what you want?

BETTY. *(Angry.)* Don't you understand, I don't know what I want! Except I just don't want this.

ROY. *(Yelling.)* Then go on! Get! I should have known when I married you that someday it would come to this. That you'd up and leave me!

BETTY. You can come with me!

ROY. You can go to hell!

BETTY. I just might! Hell would have to have a little more excitement than this place and it couldn't be any hotter!

ROY. I'll start over all by myself!

BETTY. And so will I. So long.

ROY. So long. *(There's a pause. Betty walks to the side of the stage. Roy pretends to be busy.)*

BETTY. Well ... bye, bye. I'm just going to mosey on down to where the bus used to stop and wait.

ROY. And what are you going to do for money? How do you think you're gonna buy a ticket?

BETTY. For your information, I have some money... right here in my bra. *(She pulls it out.)* It's my "mad money" for emergencies. My Mama always told me to keep a few dollars here just in case I was out on a date and I got mad at the boy... then I'd have money enough to take a bus home.

ROY. Why have you carried money there all these years?

BETTY. I guess old habits die hard. I don't know. I've never questioned why I've done anything until now.

ROY. And what makes you think a bus is coming any time soon?

BETTY. Well, if it doesn't come... then I'll just walk into the sunset. That's East, isn't it? I'm just gonna leave the past behind me... leave you behind me... *(She starts to leave... then starts to cry.)* Roy, I'm afraid.

ROY. So am I. *(He crosses and takes her in his arms. They kiss. He holds her tight.)* Oh, baby... I'll take care of you. I promise. There's no reason to be afraid. Just stop thinking about leaving. I swear it was just all those rocks. You were knocked temporarily insane. You want another Snowball? I'll go find you one. And a whole case of diet drinks. Whatever you want ... I'm gonna get it for you. I'm going to find a TV, right this minute. Once you tune in your shows you won't think about a thing. You'll be too tied up in everybody else's troubles. Now you stay right here. *(He exits.)*

BETTY. *(A pause ... then she begins to sing to herself as she looks around at the rubble. She stops... a pause, then:)* I'd better run for my life ... and God help me, if I run into a better one, I sure hope I'll know it. *(She rushes off.)*

ROY. *(Voice from off-stage.)* Betty? Wait till you see what I've found for you. *(He enters.)* See here ... it's a transistor and a Twinkie. Your favorite! Betty? *(Trying to cover his feelings.)* Come on, darlin' ... don't pull this shit on me. Come out, come out, wherever you are! Is this a game, baby? Is it like the time you dressed up in that outfit you ordered from Mr. Frederick of Hollywood and you had me chase you around and around the bedroom playing like I was "Lord of the Manor" and you were the chamber maid? Come out, come out, wherever you are! *(Pause.)* Betty, I know you have a

56

hard time telling what's real and what ain't. This is real, baby. This is home. I'll put the bathroom wherever you want it. *(Covering his pain and the fact he knows he's lost her.)* Betty? You come back before you get tired and hungry. That bus ain't ever gonna come today and the sun never will set in the East. Betty? Betty, baby. Come out, come out, wherever you are. *(A pause. He crosses and sits. He turns on the transistor radio. We hear music from the radio. Roy sits... looks out at the audience and the lights fade.)*

THE END

PROPERTY LIST — TROPICAL DEPRESSION

Table & tablecloth
2 chairs
Flower box with card
Champagne
Brochures
3 train cases
Crown
Earrings
Bathroom glass
Valium bottle
Aloha Aid
Shopping bags
Native prints
Straw mats
Fertility figure
Santos figures
Red ashtray
Chinese footstool
2 fur coats
2 beach towels
Cape
Door handle

PROPERTY LIST — TWISTER

Door
Ladder
Piece of a fence
Clothes
Other junk objects
Rocks
Snowballs
Mountain Dew
Makeup bag with lipstick, blusher & perfume

PROPERTY LIST — TWISTER

(continued)

4 women's panties
Bra
Hunting cap
Beer mug
Picture of mommy & daddy
Suspenders
Transistor radio
Twinkies

TROPICAL DEPRESSION

Song Lyrics
by Jack Heifner

LOOKING OUT AT A LOVELY SEA,
SITTING UNDER A MANGO TREE,
I WONDER WHAT COULD BE WRONG WITH ME,
THE SKY IS BLUE,
THE SEA IS TOO,
THE MANGO'S RED,
BUT IN MY HEAD,
I'VE GOT TROPICAL DEPRESSION,
AND I'VE GOT IT BAD.

NATIVE DRUMS PLAY A HAUNTING SONG,
AND NOTHING SEEMS TO BE FAR FROM WRONG,
UNLESS THE BEAT IS TO CALL KING KONG,
IT POUNDS AWAY,
BOTH NIGHT AND DAY,
IT DRIVES ME MAD,
IT MAKES ME SAD,
IT'S THIS TROPICAL DEPRESSION,
THAT I'VE GOT SO BAD.

PARADISE MAKES A PERSON THINK,
PARADISE MAKES A PERSON DRINK,
PARADISE REALLY STARTS TO STINK,
THERE'S TOO MUCH BEAT,
THERE'S TOO MUCH HEAT,
AND PARADISE CAN REALLY,
DRIVE A PERSON SILLY,
IT CAUSES TROPICAL DEPRESSION,
AND THAT'S OH SO BAD ...

OH SO BAD ...

OH SO BAD.

RECENT

 . . .

DRIVING MISS DAISY

THE MUSICAL COMEDY MURDERS OF 1940

OLD WINE IN A NEW BOTTLE

THE HANDS OF ITS ENEMY

A SHAYNA MAIDEL

STRAY DOGS

THE DELUSION OF ANGELS

MARRIAGE

THE AUTHOR'S VOICE

POPS

DISCIPLES

ROAD SHOW

THE NICE AND THE NASTY

REMEDIAL ENGLISH

Write for information as to availability

DRAMATISTS PLAY SERVICE, Inc.

440 Park Avenue South   New York, N. Y. 10016

New
PLAYS

SWEET SUE
THE COMMON PURSUIT
ELEEMOSYNARY
AMERICAN DREAMS
BOUNCERS
PHAEDRA
THE MADERATI
LILY DALE
RUNNING ON EMPTY
T BONE N WEASEL
MRS. CALIFORNIA
FUN & NOBODY
MAN DANGLING
THE WIDOW CLAIRE

Inquiries Invited

DRAMATISTS PLAY SERVICE, INC.

440 Park Avenue South　　　　　　　New York, N. Y. 10016

NEW Plays

STEEL MAGNOLIAS

THE LUCKY SPOT

THE DREAMER EXAMINES HIS PILLOW

BODIES, REST, AND MOTION

HOW TO SAY GOODBYE

JACOB'S LADDER

PASTA

MR. 80%

TRACERS

DANGER: MEMORY!

VANISHING ACT

PROGRESS

THE DREAM COAST

JITTERS

DRAMATISTS PLAY SERVICE, INC.
440 PARK AVENUE SOUTH   NEW YORK, N.Y. 10016